MW00830816

THE *Missing* SHOP MANUAL

JOINTER

THE *Missing* SHOP MANUAL

JOINTER

{ the tool information you need at your fingertips }

Distributed By
Fox Chapel Publishing

FOX CHAPEL
PUBLISHING

© 2010 by Skills Institute Press LLC
"Missing Shop Manual" series trademark of Skills Institute Press
Published and distributed in North America by Fox Chapel Publishing Company, Inc.

Jointer is an original work, first published in 2010.

Portions of text and art previously published by and reproduced under license with Direct Holdings Americas Inc.

ISBN 978-1-56523-491-8

Library of Congress Cataloging-in-Publication Data

Jointer.
    p. cm. -- (The missing shop manual)

Includes index.

ISBN: 978-1-56523-491-8

1. Woodwork--Equipment and supplies. 2. Jointer (Woodworking machine)
3. Planing-machines. I. Fox Chapel Publishing

TT186.J65 2010
684'.08--dc22

2010004499

To learn more about the other great books from Fox Chapel Publishing, or to find a retailer near you, call toll-free 800-457-9112 or visit us at
www.FoxChapelPublishing.com.

Note to Authors: We are always looking for talented authors to write new books in our area of woodworking, design, and related crafts. Please send a brief letter describing your idea to Acquisition Editor, 1970 Broad Street, East Petersburg, PA 17520.

Printed in China
First printing: September 2010

Contents

WHAT YOU WILL LEARN

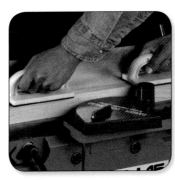

Chapter 4
Planer, page 52

Chapter 5
*Jointer & Planer
Knives,* page 62

INTRODUCTION
Jointers and Planers

The team of jointer and thickness planer are responsible for squaring the edges and faces of a workpiece. The success of any woodworking project rests on these first crucial steps, so it is essential that both machines be set up properly. Even the most accurate table saw will only compound errors made at the jointing and planing stage.

Accurate jointing depends on precise alignment of the two tables and the fence. Begin by ensuring that the outfeed table is at the same height as the cutting edges of the knives at their highest point, also known as Top Dead Center or TDC *(right)*. Then check that the tables are perfectly square to the fence and aligned with each other *(page 8)*.

Because it has more moving parts, the thickness planer requires a little more attention. Most importantly, always check

Most jointers have 90° positive stops that can be fine-tuned if the fence cannot be accurately squared to the table through normal adjustment. For the model shown (left), the 90° positive stop is a spring-loaded plunger that sits in an index collar. To fine-tune the fence position, the index collar is adjusted by means of a setscrew.

A jointer produces a smooth, even edge on a hardwood board. For best results, set a cutting depth between 1/16 and 1/8 inch.

to see that the feed rollers are properly adjusted *(page 55)* and that the planer's bed is parallel to the cutter-head along its length *(page 56)*.

Once you have designed a project and purchased the lumber, you must prepare the stock, jointing and planing it smooth and square, cutting it to the proper dimensions, and sanding any surfaces that will be difficult to reach when the work is assembled. The procedures you follow depend on how the wood was surfaced before you bought it. For rough, unsurfaced lumber, first smooth one face on the jointer, then one edge, producing two adjoining surfaces that are at 90° to each other. Next, plane the other face of the board to make it parallel to the first. When the stock is square and smooth, you are ready to rip it to width and crosscut it to length.

For S2S lumber, which has already had both faces surfaced, you need only joint one edge across the jointer, then cut to width and length. S4S stock, with all four surfaces dressed, can be ripped and crosscut immediately; only surfaces that will be glued together must be jointed. Before gluing any part of your project, remember to sand any surfaces that will be hard to reach after assembly.

CHAPTER 1:
Jointer

The jointer may seem a rather pedestrian machine compared to the table saw or band saw, but any woodworker dedicated to precision and craftsmanship will attest that using this surfacing tool properly is the first step in turning rough boards into well-built pieces of furniture.

The machine's main purpose is to shave small amounts of wood from the edges and faces of boards, yielding smooth, straight, even surfaces from which all subsequent measurements and cuts are made. The jointer gets its name from the fact that two edges run across its planing blades should fit together perfectly, forming a seamless joint.

Errors at the jointing stage of a project will have a ripple effect in all later procedures. Without a perfectly square edge to set against a table saw rip fence, for example, trimming a board to size will produce a flaw that will be further compounded when you try to cut a precise-fitting joint.

With a V-block jig clamped to the jointer infeed table, you can cut beveled edges into a workpiece accurately and safely.

Traditionally, the task of creating smooth, square edges was performed with hand planes, a painstaking process that depended on skill and experience. Nowadays, woodworkers rely on the jointer to do the job more quickly, effortlessly, and accurately. Nevertheless, it is useful to consider the workings of a hand plane when visualizing how a jointer is intended to work. The machine functions much like an inverted hand plane with somewhat larger blades driven by a motor, addressing the workpiece from below rather than above.

Although the jointer's principal role is in surfacing operations, using it for nothing more than that would be equivalent to restricting the table saw to simple cut-off work. The jointer is also useful in salvaging warped stock *(page 35)* as well as in shaping rabbets, bevels, and tapered legs *(page 41)*.

Jointers are categorized according to the length of their cutterhead knives. In practical terms, this length determines the width of the jointer's table and, more importantly, the maximum width of cut the machine can make. Sizes for consumer models range from 4 to 8 inches; 6- and 8-inch jointers are the most popular. Depth of cut, which ranges from ⅛ to ½ inch, is another distinguishing feature. But unless you plan to make frequent use of the jointer's rabbeting capability, a shallow depth of cut is adequate: The typical bite for a surfacing pass seldom exceeds ⅛ inch.

When choosing a jointer, look for a machine on which the tables on both sides of the cutterhead are adjustable. And make sure the machine has a rigid, lockable fence that can be tilted for angle cuts.

The jointer is often confused with the planer *(page 52)*, but the two machines are not interchangeable. One important function of the planer that cannot be effectively performed by a jointer is planing a surface to make it parallel to the opposite surface. Planers can also handle wider stock, important when constructing panels such as tabletops.

ANATOMY OF A JOINTER

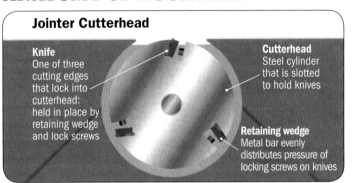

Jointer Cutterhead

Knife
One of three cutting edges that lock into cutterhead: held in place by retaining wedge and lock screws

Cutterhead
Steel cylinder that is slotted to hold knives

Retaining wedge
Metal bar evenly distributes pressure of locking screws on knives

The jointer consists of infeed and outfeed tables separated by a cylindrical cutterhead. Cutterheads typically hold three knives and rotate at several thousand revolutions per minute. For a jointer to work properly, the outfeed table must be level with the knives at the highest point of their rotation. The model illustrated on page 14-17 has an outfeed table that is adjustable to keep it at the same height as the knives. For models on which the outfeed table is fixed, the knives must be raised or lowered to bring them to the proper height.

Depth of cut is determined by the amount that the infeed table is set below the outfeed table. The fence used to guide stock over the cutterhead is normally set at a 90° angle. But on most models the fence will tilt forward or backward for cutting bevels and chamfers.

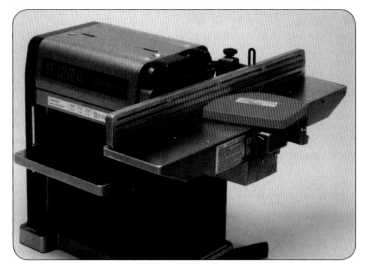

With a jointer on the right and a planer on the left, this machine combines two functions in a single appliance. The model shown can joint stock up to 6 inches wide and plane boards as wide as 12 inches.

Although the guard should always be left in place for standard operations, on most models it has to be removed for specialized work, such as rabbeting. On some machines, the guard can be installed behind the fence to provide protection during rabbeting work.

ANATOMY OF A JOINTER *(continued)*

Front View

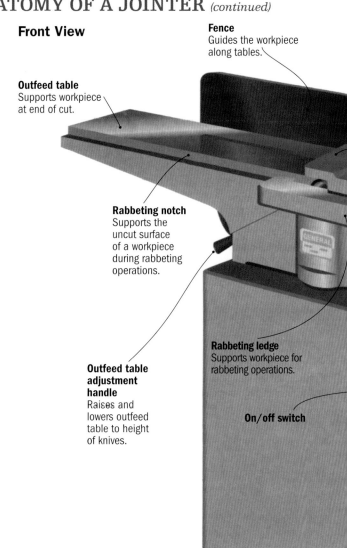

Fence
Guides the workpiece along tables.

Outfeed table
Supports workpiece at end of cut.

Rabbeting notch
Supports the uncut surface of a workpiece during rabbeting operations.

Outfeed table adjustment handle
Raises and lowers outfeed table to height of knives.

Rabbeting ledge
Supports workpiece for rabbeting operations.

On/off switch

Guard
Spring-activated plate that covers
cutterhead; protects operator from
knives. Pivoted away from cutterhead by
workpiece, it springs back into position.

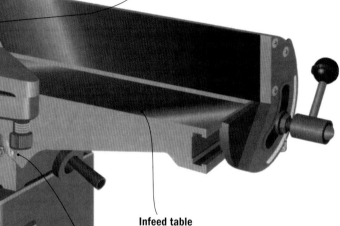

Infeed table
Supports workpiece
at the start of the cut;
height adjustable to
set depth of cut.

Depth scale
Indicates
depth of cut.

ANATOMY OF A JOINTER *(continued)*

Rear View

Fence control handle
Allows fence to be angled
45° in either direction or
moved across the tables
and cutterhead; locks
fence in fixed positions.

Fence stop
Setscrew and metal stop
hold the fence vertical
or in its most frequently
used angled settings.

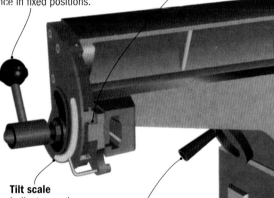

Tilt scale
Indicates angle
of the fence.

**Infeed table
adjustment handle**
Raises and lowers
infeed table to set
depth of cut.

ANATOMY OF A JOINTER *(continued)*

Gib screw
Adjustable to keep tables parallel to each other and in same horizontal plane; model shown has three such screws on each side of pulley cover.

Pulley cover

Friction knob
Tightened to keep table from slipping from selected height setting.

SETTING OUTFEED TABLE HEIGHT

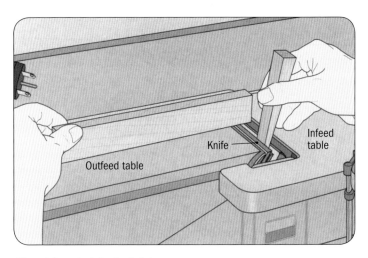

Checking table height

Use a small wooden wedge to rotate the cutterhead until the edge of one of the knives is at its highest point. Then hold a straight hardwood board on the outfeed table so that it extends over the cutterhead without contacting the infeed table *(above)*. The knife should just brush against the board. Perform the test along the length of the knife, moving the board from the fence to the rabbeting ledge. Repeat the test for the other knives. If one knife fails the test, adjust its height as you would when installing a blade. If none of the knives touch the board, adjust the height of the outfeed table.

SETTING OUTFEED
TABLE HEIGHT *(continued)*

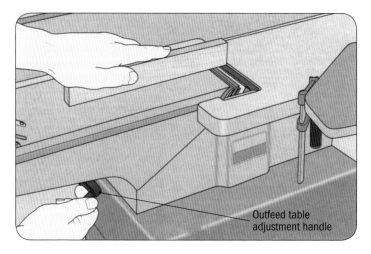

Outfeed table
adjustment handle

Adjusting the outfeed table height

Keeping the hardwood board over the cutterhead, turn the outfeed table adjustment handle *(above)*, raising or lowering the table until the edge of a knife just brushes against the board. Then check the table height in relation to the other knives.

SETTING OUTFEED
TABLE HEIGHT *(continued)*

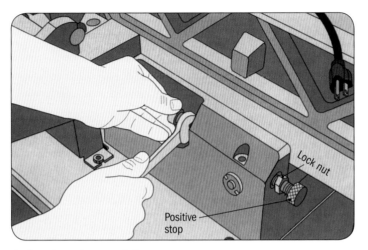

Adjusting the positive stop

If the outfeed table is still not level with the knives, adjust the jointer's positive stops, which prevent the table from moving out of alignment while in use. For the model shown, first tighten the outfeed table lock and loosen the two lock nuts on the other side of the tool. Back off the two positive stops and then adjust the height of the outfeed table with the adjustment handle until the table is level with the knives at their highest point of rotation. Tighten the table lock. Tighten the positive stops as far as they will go, then tighten the lock nuts *(above)*.

SETTING OUTFEED
TABLE HEIGHT *(continued)*

One of the most common jointing and planing defects is snipe, or a concave cut at the trailing end of a workpiece. On a planer, snipe occurs when there is too much play between the table and the feed rollers, and can be corrected by proper feedroller adjustment (page 55). On a jointer (above), snipe occurs when the outfeed table is set lower than the knives at their highest point of rotation, and can be corrected by aligning the outfeed table (page 20).

ALIGNING THE TABLES AND FENCE

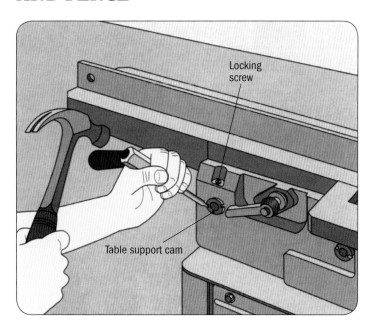

Locking screw

Table support cam

Aligning the tables

Remove the jointer's fence, then raise the infeed table to the same height as the outfeed table. Use a straightedge to confirm that the two tables are absolutely level. If the alignment is not perfect, adjust the horizontal position of the tables. The model shown features eccentric table supports that can be adjusted by first loosening a locking screw and then tapping an adjustment cam with a hammer and screwdriver *(above)*.

ALIGNING THE TABLES
AND FENCE *(continued)*

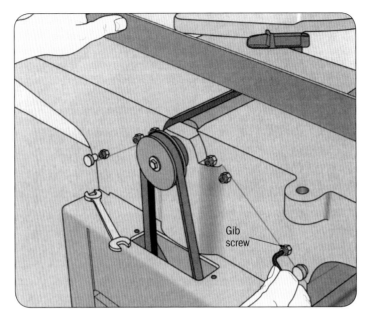

Gib
screw

When the tables are perfectly level, tighten the locking screws. If you
have a jointer with gib screws, adjust one or more of the gib screws at
the back of the tool until the straightedge rests flush on both tables
(above); remove the pulley cover, if necessary, to access the screws.
If you moved the outfeed table during this process, recheck its height.

SETTING UP AND SAFETY

Accurate jointing depends on precise alignment of the two tables and the fence—the parts of the machine that guide a workpiece into and over the knives. Begin by ensuring that the outfeed table is at the same height as the cutting edges of the knives at their highest point. Then check that the tables are perfectly square to the fence and aligned properly with each other.

Before starting, make sure that the jointer is unplugged and install a clamp on the rabbeting ledge to hold the guard temporarily out of your way.

Once you have the machine properly tuned, pause and consider safety. The knives of a spinning cutterhead look seductively benign. It is easy to forget that this harmless-looking blur can cause as much damage to fingers and hands as can a table saw blade. Resist the temptation to operate the jointer without the guard in place. When the guard must be removed from its normal position in front of the fence for rabbeting operations, install it behind the fence if your jointer is set up for such a switch.

Even with the guard in place, always keep your hands away from the knives. When jointing the edge of a board, your hands should ride along the workpiece, rather than on the tables. When face-jointing, always use push blocks to feed a workpiece across the knives. Whatever the cut, remember to press the workpiece firmly against the tables and fence.

JOINTER SAFETY TIPS

- Check regularly to make sure that the knives are sharp and securely fastened to the cutterhead.

- Unplug the jointer while installing knives or performing any setup operation.

- Wear appropriate safety glasses and hearing protection when operating the jointer.

- Do not joint stock with loose knots, or the workpiece may catch in the cutterhead.

- Never joint stock that is less than 12 inches long.

- Do not face-joint stock that is less than ⅜ inch thick.

- Do not joint the end grain of a workpiece that is less than 6 inches wide.

- When the machine is running, keep your hands out of the area 4 inches above and to either side of the jointer's cutterhead.

- Never reach up into the dust chute unless the jointer is unplugged.

SETTING THE KNIFE HEIGHT

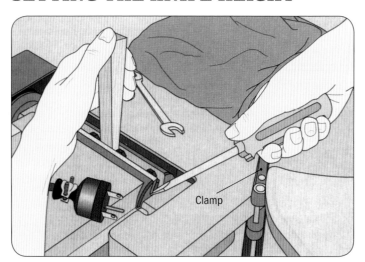

Clamp

Cover the edge of the knife with a rag and partially tighten each lock screw in turn; then tighten them fully, beginning with the ones in the center and working out to the edges. Check the outfeed table height *(page 18)* in relation to the knife just installed. If the knife is set too low, loosen the lock screws slightly, then pry up the knife using a screwdriver *(above)* while holding the cutterhead stationary with a wedge; if it is too high, tap it down using a wood block. Tighten the lock screws and remove the clamp from the rabbeting ledge.

USING A KNIFE-SETTING JIG

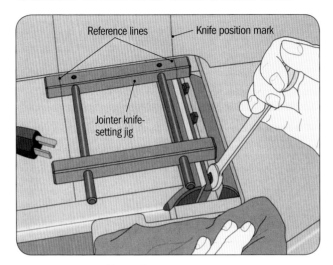

Reference lines

Knife position mark

Jointer knife-setting jig

Setting the knife height

Remove an old knife and install a new one *(page 70)*. Use a small wedge to rotate the cutterhead until the edge of the new knife is at its highest point. Then mark a line on the fence directly above the cutting edge using a square and a pencil. Position the knife-setting jig on the outfeed table, aligning the reference line on the jig arm with the marked line on the fence, as shown. Mark another line on the fence directly above the second reference line on the jig arm. Remove the jig and extend this line across the outfeed table. (The line will help you quickly position the jig the next time you install a knife.) Reposition the jig on the table, aligning its reference lines with the marked lines on the fence. Then use a wrench to tighten the lock screws *(above)*. Remove the clamp from the rabbeting ledge.

CHAPTER 2:

Jointing

One of the first rules of jointing is that a workpiece should always be fed across the cutterhead so the knives are cutting with the grain. You will get the smoothest cut while reducing the risk of splintering or kickback. If the grain turns in a workpiece, feed the stock so most of the cut is following the grain.

The sequence for jointing operations should depend on the wood you are using. For rough lumber, joint the faces first, then do the edges. For wood on which both faces have already been surfaced, jointing the edges is usually sufficient.

In general, set a cutting depth of $\frac{1}{8}$ inch for softwoods or $\frac{1}{16}$ inch for hardwoods. Always use a push block to face-joint. Whatever the depth you select, check the setting before making the first pass. Unplug the jointer and use a scrap of wood to rotate the cutterhead so that all the knives are below the level of the tables. Then, place a board flush on the outfeed table; the gap between the board's edge and the infeed table will equal the depth of cut.

If most of your jointing involves working with board edges, avoid dulling the same narrow segment of your knives by routinely moving the fence over slightly to evenly distribute the wear.

JOINTING AN EDGE

Feeding a workpiece into the cut

Lay the workpiece on the infeed table a few inches from the knives, butting its face against the fence. Slowly feed the workpiece into the cutterhead knives *(right)*, pressing it against the fence with your left hand while moving it steadily forward with your right hand. As the workpiece crosses to the outfeed table, gradually shift your weight from your back foot to your front foot. Continue feeding the stock until your right hand approaches the outfeed table.

Finishing the pass

When your right hand reaches the outfeed table, reverse the position of your hands while continuing to feed the workpiece. Gradually slide your left hand toward the back of the workpiece *(right)*, maintaining pressure against the fence. Then shift your right hand further back on the stock to maintain downward pressure just to the outfeed side of the knives. Continue these hand-over-hand movements until the pass is completed.

JOINTING END GRAIN

Making a partial pass

Place the workpiece end-down on the infeed table a few inches from the knives with its face flat against the fence. Straddle the fence with your right hand and wrap your thumb around the workpiece to feed it slowly into the cutterhead. Stop feeding about one inch into the pass and immediately tilt the workpiece back away from the knives as shown.

Reversing the workpiece and completing the pass

Turn the workpiece 180° and slowly feed the stock across the knives *(right)*, straddling the fence with your right hand while maintaining pressure with your left hand. The partial pass made before should prevent splintering at the end of this pass.

JOINTING A FACE

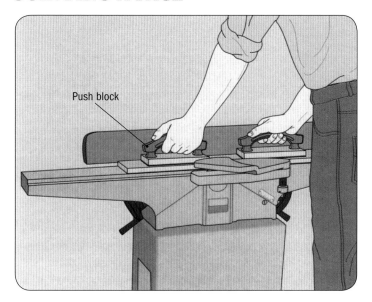

Push block

Using push blocks

Move the fence toward the rabbeting ledge, if necessary, so no portion of the knives will be exposed as the workpiece passes over the cutterhead. Lay the workpiece face-down on the infeed table a few inches from the knives, butting its edge against the fence. Then put two push blocks squarely on top of the stock, centered between its edges. (Use push blocks with angled handles to keep your hands from hitting the fence.) Slowly feed the workpiece across the knives *(above)* applying downward pressure on the outfeed side of the knives to keep the stock flat on the tables and lateral pressure to keep it flush against the fence. For a long workpiece, bring your left hand to the back of the workpiece when your right hand reaches the outfeed table.

JOINTING A FACE *(continued)*

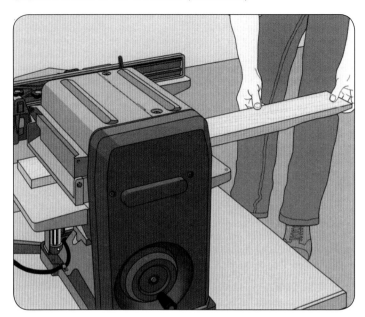

Planing stock

Set a cutting depth up to 1/16 inch. Stand to one side of the planer and use both hands to feed the stock carefully into the machine, keeping the board edges parallel to the edges of the planer table. Once the machine grips the board and begins pulling it across the cutterhead, support the trailing end to keep it flat on the table *(above)*. As the cut progresses, move to the outfeed side of the planer and support the piece with both hands until it clears the outfeed roller. If you are making several passes to reduce the board's thickness, plane the same amount of wood from both faces. This will minimize warping.

OUTFEED TABLE ALIGNMENT

Poor results with a jointer can often be attributed to misalignment of the outfeed table in relation to the cutterhead. Perfect jointing depends on the tables being at precisely the same height as the knives *(page 8)*. The diagrams above illustrate what can go wrong if the outfeed table is too high or too low—and what should happen when it is at the correct height. If the outfeed table is set higher than the knives, jointing will produce a taper *(right, top)*; if the table is too low, the blades will leave a concave cut, called a snipe, at the end of the workpiece *(right, center)*. When the table is properly adjusted the result will be a smooth, even cut *(right, bottom)*.

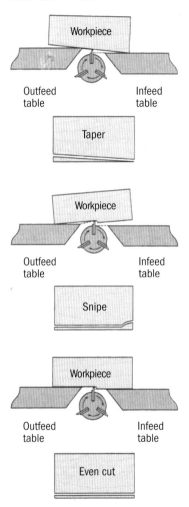

A PUSH BLOCK

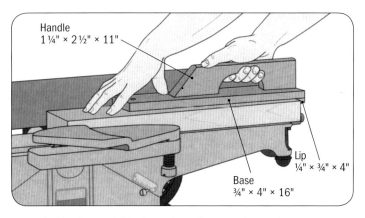

Handle
1 ¼" × 2 ½" × 11"

Lip
¼" × ¾" × 4"

Base
¾" × 4" × 16"

Instead of buying push blocks such as the ones shown above, some woodworkers prefer to make their own. Refer to the illustration at right for suggested dimensions, although you can tailor your design to the workpiece at hand.

Glue the lip to the underside of the base, flush with one end. Then position the handle on the top of the base so its back end is flush with the end of the base. Screw the handle to the base, driving the screws from the underside of the base. Countersink the screws to avoid scratching the workpiece when you use the push block. Bore a hole near the front end of the base so you can hang the push block on the wall when it is not in use.

Use the push block as described above, but position it on the workpiece so the lip hugs the trailing end of the stock. Position your left hand on the workpiece near its front end, bracing your thumb on the push block.

CONVEX AND CONCAVE EDGES

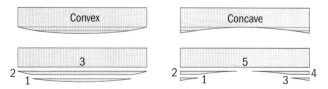

Although the jointer's principal value rests in its ability to smooth and square rough wood surfaces, it can also straighten out stock with other defects. It is especially useful for evening out boards that have concave (inward-bowing) or convex (outward-bowing) faces. The diagrams above show how to correct both types of irregularities.

In each operation, the high spots on the wood surface are passed repeatedly across the cutterhead until they are removed. For a convex edge *(above, left)*, pass the high spot at the middle of the board repeatedly across the cutterhead as many times as necessary *(cuts 1 and 2)*. Try not to "nose-dive" or to allow the leading edge to ride up while you are cutting. When the surface is roughly even, make a final pass along the entire edge *(cut 3)*.

For a concave edge, pass the high spot at one end of the board across the knives *(above, right)* as many times as necessary *(cuts 1 and 2)*, then turn the board around to repeat the process at the other end *(cuts 3 and 4)*. When the surface is roughly even, make a final pass *(cut 5)*.

JOINTING A CURVED EDGE

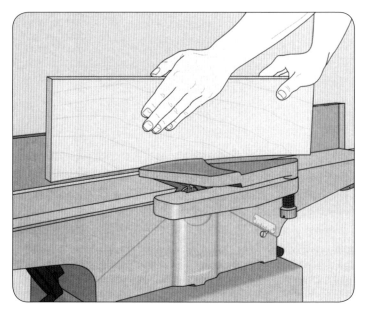

Trimming concave and convex edges

To straighten an edge with a concave curve, hold the leading end of the workpiece an inch or so above table level in front of the cutterhead guard. Feed the workpiece with your right hand; use your left hand to maintain pressure against the fence. When the deepest part of the concave edge is over the cutterhead *(above)*, lower the leading end of the workpiece onto the outfeed table and complete the pass. Continue feeding the workpiece past the cutterhead until the trailing end is straight. Then turn the workpiece 180° and repeat the procedure for the other end of the board. Make a final pass along the entire edge. For a convex curve, make a pass over the blades as you would for a standard jointing operation, keeping the workpiece as parallel as possible to the jointer tables. Keep making shallow passes through the jointer until the edge is true.

SALVAGING WARPED LUMBER

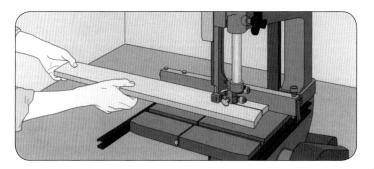

Ripping cupped stock into narrow boards

Using a bandsaw set the width of cut; the narrower the setting, the flatter the resulting boards. To make a cut, set the board convex (high) side up on the table and, butting the board against the fence, feed it steadily into the blade *(above)*. Make sure that neither hand is in line with the cutting edge. Finish the cut with a push stick. Remove any remaining high spots on the jointer *(page 36)*.

---

*Shop*Tip

Jointing wide boards
If you have boards that are too cumbersome to move across the jointer, you can undertake the task with a router and a perfectly square edge guide. Install a ½-inch toppiloted flush-trimming bit in a router with a ½-inch collet. Position the edge guide atop the board to be jointed and clamp the pieces to a work-bench with the edge of the board protruding from the guide's edge by about ⅟₁₆ inch. Feed the router from one end of the board to the other; the pilot will ride along the guide as the cutter trims the board flush.

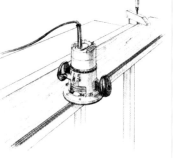

JOINTING ON A ROUTER TABLE

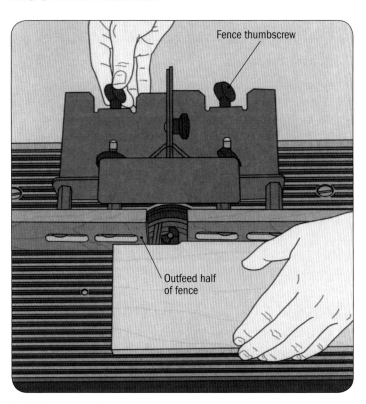

Fence thumbscrew

Outfeed half
of fence

Jointing an edge

Install a straight bit in the router with a cutting edge longer than the
thickness of your workpiece, and mount the tool in a router table.
To remove $\frac{1}{16}$ inch of wood from your stock—a typical amount when
jointing—adjust the position of the fence for a cut of that amount.
Make a test cut in a scrap board, then unplug the router and hold
the board in place against the fence. Loosen the outfeed fence

JOINTING ON A
ROUTER TABLE *(continued)*

thumbscrews and advance the outfeed half until it butts against the cut part of the board *(above, left)*. Tighten the thumbscrews. Butt the workpiece against the fence a few inches back from the bit and then slowly feed the board into the cutter, keeping your hand clear of the bit and pressing the workpiece firmly against the fence *(above, right)*. Apply side pressure just to the outfeed side of the bit. For narrow stock, finish the cut with a push stick.

CHAPTER 3:

Rabbets, Chamfers, & Tapers

With a little resourcefulness, you can do more than produce square boards on a jointer. By taking full advantage of the machine's capabilities, you can shape wood with tapers and chamfers, or even cut rabbets for joinery. In fact, many woodworkers consider the jointer the best tool for cutting rabbets—at least when you are working with the grain of a workpiece.

As long as your jointer has a rabbeting ledge, it can cut rabbets along either the edge or the face of a board. Since the guard must be removed for edge rabbets on stock thicker than ¾ inch and for any rabbet along the face of a board, extra caution is essential.

Angled cuts along the corners of a workpiece, known as chamfers, are made on the jointer by tilting the fence to the required angle or with the aid of a shop-made jig. Tapers are also straightforward. With a stop block clamped to each table, you can cut stopped tapers that leave square ends for joining to a tabletop or seat, or for carving into a decorative foot.

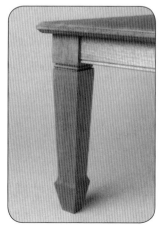

A leg tapered on the jointer provides graceful support for this table.

RABBETING ON THE JOINTER

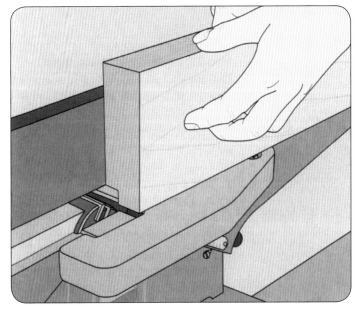

Cutting rabbets

Mark cutting lines for the width and depth of the rabbet on the leading end of the workpiece. Align the width mark with the ends of the knives, then position the fence flush against the workpiece. Set the cutting depth no deeper than ¼ inch. For a rabbet along a board edge *(above)*, feed the workpiece from above with your right hand while your left hand maintains pressure against the fence. Increase the cutting depth by increments no deeper than ¼ inch and make additional passes if necessary.

RABBETING ON
THE JOINTER *(continued)*

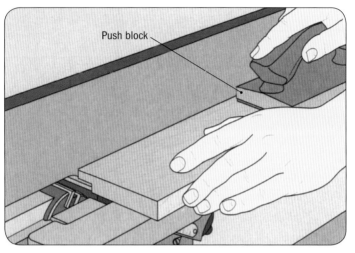

Push block

For a rabbet along a board face *(above)*, guide the workpiece near its front end with your left hand, while using a push block to apply downward pressure and keep the workpiece flat on the tables. Slowly feed the workpiece across the knives, then deepen the rabbet, if necessary.

MAKING A SIMPLE TAPER

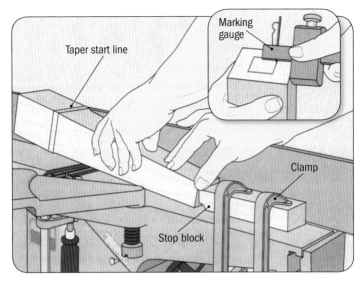

Marking gauge

Taper start line

Clamp

Stop block

Setting up and starting the cut

Use a marking gauge to outline the taper on the workpiece *(inset)*; then mark lines on the four faces of the stock to indicate where the taper will begin. Install a clamp on the rabbeting ledge to hold the guard out of the way. Set a ⅛-inch depth of cut and, holding the workpiece against the fence, align the taper start line with the front of the outfeed table. Butt a stop block against the other end of the workpiece and clamp it to the infeed table. To start each pass, carefully lower the workpiece onto the knives while holding the workpiece firmly against the fence and making sure that your hands are on the infeed side of the knives *(top)*. Straddle the fence with your right hand, using your thumb to keep the workpiece flush against the stop block.

MAKING A SIMPLE TAPER *(continued)*

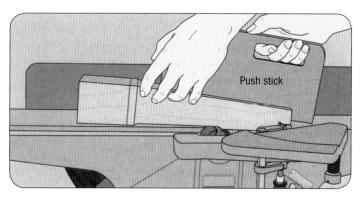

Push stick

Cutting the taper

Use a push stick to feed the workpiece across the cutterhead. With
your right hand, apply downward pressure on the trailing end of the
workpiece; use your left hand to keep the workpiece flush against the
fence *(above)*. Make as many passes across the knives as necessary
to complete the taper on the first face of the workpiece. To cut the
remaining faces, rotate the workpiece clockwise 90° and make
repeated passes over the cutterhead until you have trimmed the stock
down to the taper marks.

JOINTING A STOPPED TAPER

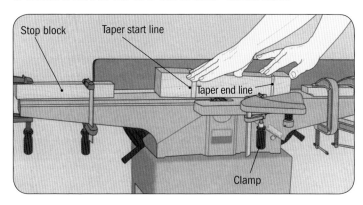

Stop block — Taper start line — Taper end line — Clamp

Cutting with twin stop blocks

Mark lines on all faces of the workpiece to indicate where the tapering
will begin and end. Install a clamp on the rabbeting ledge to hold the
guard out of the way. Set a ⅛-inch depth of cut, then butt the workpiece
against the fence with the taper start line ¾ inch behind the front of the
outfeed table. (The extra ¾ inch will compensate for the fact that when
the infeed table is lowered later, it will also slide back slightly.) Butt a
stop block against the end of the workpiece and clamp it to the infeed
table. Next, align the taper end line with the back end of the infeed
table. Butt a second stop block against the other end of the workpiece
and clamp in place. To make the first pass, lower the workpiece onto
the knives, keeping it flush against the fence and the stop block on the
infeed table. Feed the workpiece using the thumb of your right hand
(above), fingers straddling the fence; use your left hand to press the
workpiece against the fence and down on the knives. Keep both hands
well above the cutterhead. Make one pass on each face, then lower the
infeed table ⅛ inch and repeat the process on all four sides. Continue,
increasing the cutting depth until the taper is completed.

MAKING PENCIL POSTS

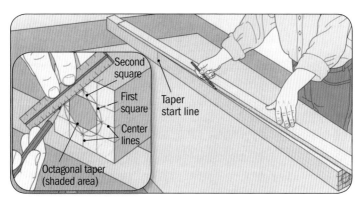

Second square
First square
Taper start line
Center lines
Octagonal taper (shaded area)

Outlining the tapers

For a bed of the dimensions shown on page 50, mark a line for the start of the taper all around the blank 20 inches from the bottom end. Then outline the octagonal taper on the center of the top end. Start by centering a 1¼-inch square on the end with sides parallel to the stock's side. Extend the sides of the square to the edges of the stock, then draw vertical and horizontal lines through the center, each bisecting the square's sides. Next use a compass to draw a circle from the center of the square that passes through each of its four corners. Then, with a pencil and ruler, draw a second square whose corners meet where the circle and center lines intersect *(inset)*. The octagonal shape will be cut by first tapering the stock to the dimensions of the first square you drew, then by planing the corners of that square down to the remaining sides of the second square. Mark the first cuts by using a pencil and long straightedge to extend the taper lines from the end to the start line *(above)*.

MAKING PENCIL POSTS *(continued)*

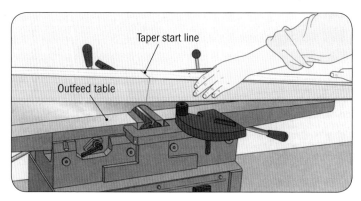

Taper start line

Outfeed table

Setting up and starting the taper

An easy way to taper the posts is with a jointer. Set the machine for a shallow cut and position the fence to expose only about 4 inches of the cutterhead. For this operation, also adjust the guard out of the way. Then, holding the blank against the fence, align the taper start line with the front of the outfeed table. To start each pass, carefully lower the blank onto the cutterhead while holding it firmly against the fence *(above)*. Make sure both hands are over the infeed side of the table.

MAKING PENCIL POSTS *(continued)*

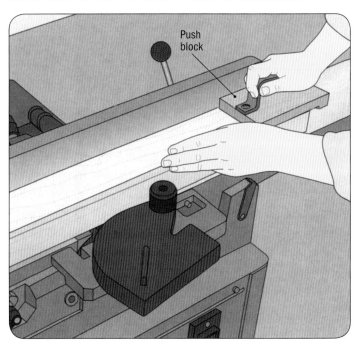

Push
block

Tapering the posts

Feed the leg across the cutterhead with a push block, pressing down
on the trailing end of the stock while holding it flush against the fence
(above). Keep your left hand away from the cutterhead. Make as many
passes as necessary until you have trimmed the stock to the taper
outline, repeating the process to shape the remaining faces. If your
markings are correct, you should make the same number of passes on
each side. Clean up the taper at the start line using a belt sander.

BEVELING TAPERS

Laying out the bevels

To form the octagon, bevel the corners of the square taper. The bevel is already outlined on the end of each post, but it must also be marked on the sides of the stock. Taking the dimensions from a piece of full-size post stock, and drawing on scrap plywood, outline squares as you did before *(right, top)*. Transfer your measurement—equal to the bevel width—to the post, measuring from each corner of the square to either side. Then use a pencil and a long straightedge to connect each mark with its corresponding point on the octagon drawn at the top end of each post. Once all eight bevel lines are marked, draw a curved lamb's tongue at each corner, joining the bevel marks with the taper start line *(right, bottom)*.

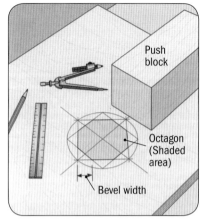

Push block

Octagon (Shaded area)

Bevel width

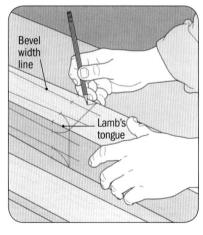

Bevel width line

Lamb's tongue

BEVELING TAPERS *(continued)*

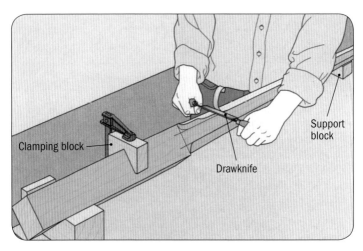

Clamping block

Support block

Drawknife

Roughing out the bevels

To secure the posts, use three wood blocks. Cut V-shaped notches into an edge of each one, then place two of the blocks under the workpiece to support it and clamp one on top between the other two; position two of the blocks around the square portion of the post. Then use a drawknife to shape the tapered portion of the posts into octagons, beveling one corner at a time. Holding the drawknife on the stock bevel-side down, pull the tool toward the top end of the post *(above)*. The depth of cut depends on how much you tilt the handles; the lower the angle, the shallower the cut. Take a light shaving, always following the wood grain.

BEVELING TAPERS *(continued)*

A V-Block Jig

To cut a series of chamfers on the jointer, use this simple shop-made jig. Refer to the illustration shown at right for suggested dimensions.

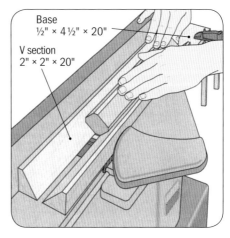

Base
½" × 4½" × 20"

V section
2" × 2" × 20"

Begin the V section of the jig by bevel cutting 2-by-2s. Position the two cut pieces so that they extend beyond one end of the base by about 6 inches, and have a ½-inch gap between them. Attach the two pieces through the base with countersunk screws to avoid scratching the jointer table when the jig is clamped in place.

To use the jig, clamp it in place with one end of the base aligned with the cutterhead-end of the infeed table. Lower the infeed table to the maximum depth of cut, typically ½ inch. Seat the workpiece in the gap of the jig, then feed it across the knives with your right hand, while holding it firmly in the V with your left hand.

CHAPTER 4

Planer

For smoothing rough stock, planing a glued-up panel, or reducing the thickness of a board uniformly, the planer is the ideal woodworking machine. Its main function is to produce a smooth surface that is parallel to the opposite face.

Planers are easy to use, but keep the following points in mind to get the best results. Always feed stock into the knives following the direction of grain. Limit each pass to 1/16 inch and make multiple passes.

Some of the tasks you perform on the jointer cannot be duplicated on the planer. For example, since the planer produces parallel surfaces, warped stock will emerge from the machine thinner, but just as warped.

HOW A PLANER WORKS

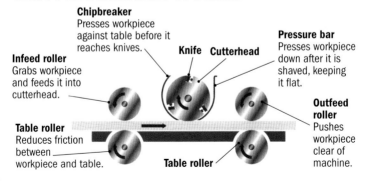

Chipbreaker
Presses workpiece against table before it reaches knives.

Knife **Cutterhead**

Pressure bar
Presses workpiece down after it is shaved, keeping it flat.

Infeed roller
Grabs workpiece and feeds it into cutterhead.

Outfeed roller
Pushes workpiece clear of machine.

Table roller
Reduces friction between workpiece and table.

Table roller

PLANING A BOARD

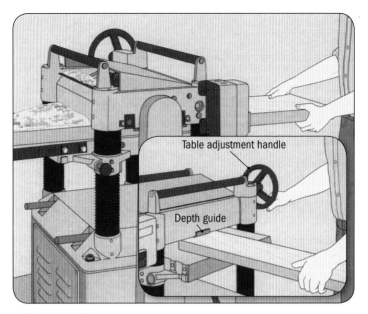

Table adjustment handle

Depth guide

Using the planer

To set the cutting depth, lay the workpiece on the table and align its end with the depth guide. For a typical 1/16-inch depth of cut, turn the table adjustment handle until the top of the board just clears the bottom of the guide *(inset)*. To make a pass through the planer, stand to one side of the workpiece and use both hands to feed it slowly into the infeed roller, keeping its edges parallel to the table edges. Once the infeed roller grips the workpiece and begins pulling it past the cutterhead, support the trailing end of the stock to keep it flat on the table *(above)*. As the trailing end of the workpiece reaches the planer's table, move to the outfeed side of the machine. Support the workpiece with both hands until it clears the outfeed roller. To prevent stock from warping, plane from both sides of a workpiece rather than removing thickness from one side only.

PLANERS

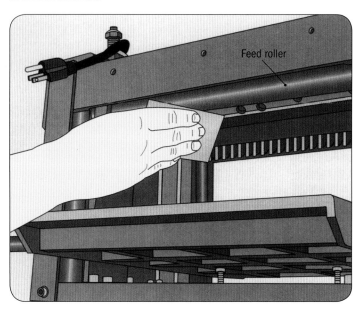

Feed roller

Cleaning planer rollers

Planer feed rollers can get dirty quickly when planing pitch-filled softwoods such as pine. Periodically use mineral spirits or a solution of ammonia and water with a brass-bristled brush to clean metal feed rollers of pitch and resin. Clean rubber feed rollers with a sharp cabinet scraper *(above)*.

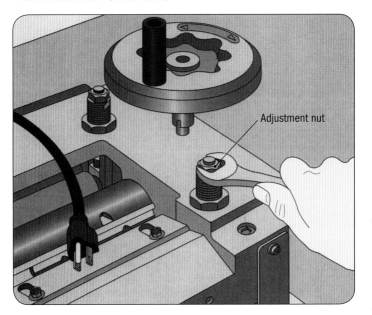

Adjustment nut

Adjusting feed rollers

Sometimes it is necessary to increase pressure on a planer's feed rollers, as when planing narrow stock, or when stock slips as it is fed into the machine. In either case, the infeed roller should firmly grip the board. (Some planers feature a serrated metal infeed roller; in this case the pressure should be enough to move the board but not so much that the rollers leave a serrated pattern in the board after it is planed.) On most planers, the feed rollers are adjusted by turning spring-loaded screws on top of the machine. For the model shown, remove the plastic caps and adjust the hex nuts with an open-end wrench *(above)*. Make sure after adjusting the feed rollers that the table is parallel to the rollers *(page 56)*. If the rollers do not carry the wood smoothly through the planer after adjustments, clean the rollers or wax the table.

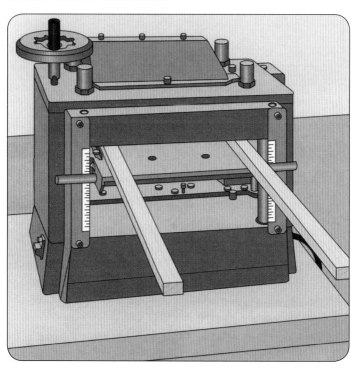

Checking the table for level

To check if your planer's table is level and parallel to the cutterhead, run two jointed strips of wood of the same thickness through opposite sides of the machine *(above)*, then compare the resulting thicknesses. If there is a measurable difference, adjust the table according to the manufacturer's instructions. If your model of planer has no such adjustment, reset the knives in the cutterhead so they are slightly lower at the lower end of the table to compensate for the error.

PLANERS *(continued)*

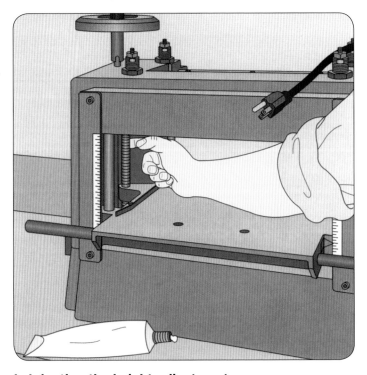

Lubricating the height adjustment

To ensure smooth operation, periodically clean the planer's height
adjustment mechanism, first using a clean, dry cloth to remove sawdust
and grease. Then lubricate the threads with a Teflon™-based lubricant
or automotive bearing grease; oil should be avoided as it may stain
the wood.

PLANING SHORT AND THIN STOCK

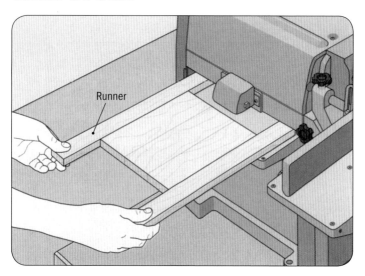

Runner

Using runner guides to plane short stock

Feeding short boards through a thickness planer can cause sniping and kickback. To hold short stock steady as it enters and exits the planer, glue two solid wood scrap runners to the edges of your workpiece. Make sure the runners are the same thickness as the workpiece and extend several inches beyond both ends. Feed the workpiece into the planer *(above)*, making a series of light cuts until you reach the desired thickness. Then cut off the runners.

PLANING SHORT AND
THIN STOCK *(continued)*

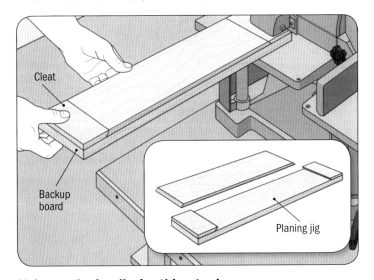

Cleat

Backup board

Planing jig

Using a planing jig for thin stock

Thickness planing stock thinner than ¼ inch often causes chatter and splintering of the workpiece. To avoid these problems, make thin stock "thicker" with this jig. Simply glue two beveled cleats to either end of a board that is slightly longer than your workpiece *(inset)*. To make the cleats, cut a 45° bevel across the middle of a board approximately the same thickness as the workpiece. Next, bevel the ends of the workpiece. Set the stock on a backup board, position the cleats flush against the workpiece so the bevel cuts are in contact, and glue the cleats in place to the backup board. Run the jig and workpiece through the planer, making several light passes down to the desired thickness *(above)*, then crosscut the ends of the workpiece square.

PLANING SHORT AND THIN STOCK *(continued)*

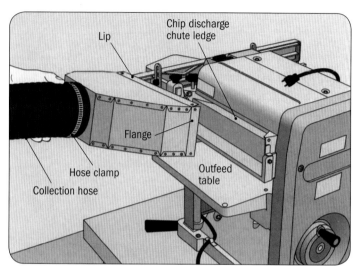

Labels: Lip · Chip discharge chute ledge · Flange · Hose clamp · Collection hose · Outfeed table

Hooking a planer up to the dust-control system

A hood like the one shown above can be custom-built to capture most of the dust generated by your planer. Make the hood from galvanized sheet metal, cutting the pieces with tin snips. Leave tabs where the pieces overlap so they can be pop riveted together. Make flanges on the sides to improve the seal and a hole in the back for the dust collection hose; you will also need to create a lip along the top to connect to the ledge of the planer's chip discharge chute. Use an adapter to join the hood to the hose, inserting one end in the hole in the hood and the other end in the hose; reinforce the connection with a hose clamp. Fasten the lip of the hood to the planer with sheet metal screws.

TOOL PLACEMENT
AND WORK FLOW

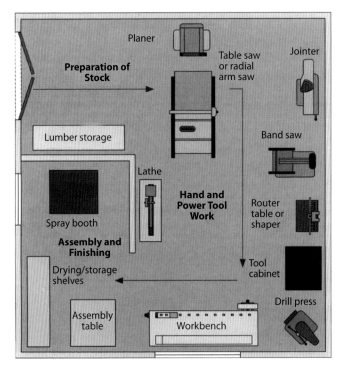

Designing a shop around the woodworking process

For maximum efficiency, lay out the tools in your shop so the
lumber follows a fairly direct route from rough stock to finished pieces.
The diagram above illustrates a logical work flow for a medium-size
workshop. At the upper left-hand corner is the entrance where lumber is
stored on racks. To the right is the stock preparation area, devoted to the
table saw (or radial arm saw), jointer, and planer; at this station, lumber
is cut to rough length and surfaced.

CHAPTER 5:

Jointer & Planer Knives

Unlike the blades of other woodworking machines, whose height and angle are adjustable, jointer knives are designed to function at just one setting: parallel to and at the same height as the machine's outfeed table. As such, the height of all the knives must be identical; a difference of as little as a fraction of an inch can compromise the jointer's ability to produce smooth, square edges.

Like all blades, jointer knives work well only when they are sharp. However, because removing a jointer knife for sharpening and then reinstalling it properly can be a time consuming operation, many woodworkers go to great lengths to avoid changing these blades. There are tricks you can use to prolong the useful life of a set of knives.

A pair of magnetic jigs holds a planer knife at the correct height in the cutterhead, allowing the knife to be fixed in place accurately. Such jigs take the guesswork out of the trickiest phase of sharpening planer knives—installing them properly. Periodic sharpening of planer knives is essential. Stock surfaced by dull knives is difficult to glue and does not accept finishes well. A similar jig is available for setting jointer knives.

HONING JOINTER KNIVES

Cleaning the knives

Jointer knives can be honed while they are in the cutterhead. Start
by cleaning them. Shift the fence away from the tables and move the
guard out of the way. Making sure the jointer is unplugged, rotate the
cutterhead with a stick until one of the knives is at the highest point in
its rotation. Then, holding the cutterhead steady with one hand protected
by a rag, use a small brass-bristled brush soaked in solvent to clean the
knife *(above)*. Repeat for the other knives.

HONING JOINTER KNIVES *(continued)*

Aligning the infeed table with the knives

Cut a piece of ¼-inch plywood to the width of the jointer's infeed table and secure it to the table with double-faced tape. The plywood will protect the table from scratches when you hone the knives. Next, adjust the infeed table so the beveled edge of the knives is at the same level as the top of the plywood. Set a straight board on the plywood and across the cutterhead and, holding the cutterhead steady with the beveled edge of one knife parallel to the table, lower the infeed table until the bottom of the board contacts the bevel *(above)*. Use a wood shim to wedge the cutterhead in place.

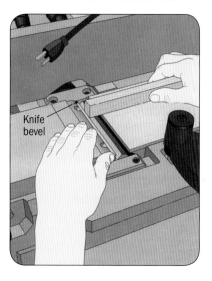

Knife bevel

HONING JOINTER KNIVES *(continued)*

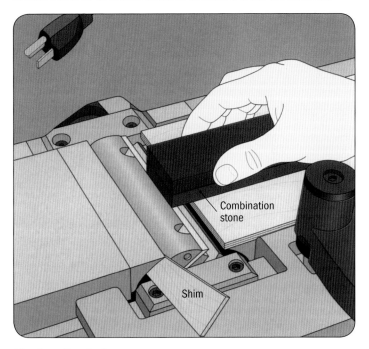

Combination stone

Shim

Honing the knives

Slide a combination stone evenly across the beveled edge of the knife *(above)*. Move the stone with a side-to-side motion until the bevel is flat and sharp, avoiding contact with the cutterhead. Repeat the process to hone the remaining knives.

SHARPENING JOINTER KNIVES

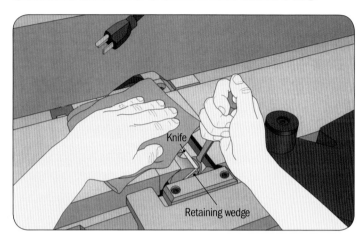

Removing the knives

To give jointer knives a full-fledged sharpening, remove them from the cutterhead. Unplug the machine, shift the fence away from the tables, and move the guard out of the way. Use a small wood scrap to rotate the cutterhead until the lock screws securing one of the knives are accessible between the tables. Cover the edge of the knife with a rag to protect your hands, then use a wrench to loosen each screw *(above)*. Lift the knife and the retaining wedge out of the cutterhead.

SHARPENING JOINTER
KNIVES *(continued)*

Cleaning the retaining wedge

Clean any pitch or gum from the retaining wedge using a brass-bristled brush dipped in solvent *(right, top)*. If the face of the retaining wedge that butts against the knife is pitted or rough, you may have trouble setting the knife height when reinstalling the knife. Use the brush to clean the slot in the cutterhead that houses the retaining wedge and knife *(right, bottom)*.

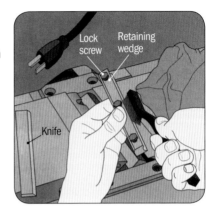

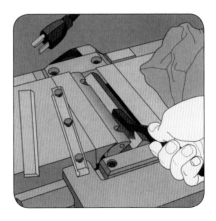

SHARPENING JOINTER
KNIVES *(continued)*

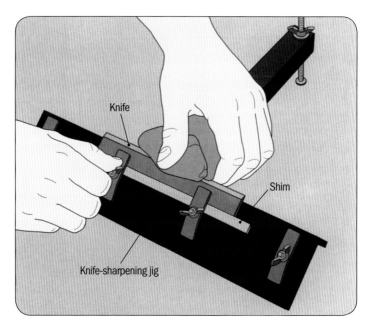

Knife

Shim

Knife-sharpening jig

Installing the knife in a sharpening jig

Use a commercial knife-sharpening jig to sharpen the jointer knife.
Center the knife in the jig bevel up and clamp it in place by tightening
the wing nuts; use a rag to protect your hand *(above)*. Make sure that
the blade is parallel with the lip of the jig. If the knife does not extend
out far enough from the jig, insert a wood shim between the knife and
the jig clamps.

SHARPENING JOINTER
KNIVES *(continued)*

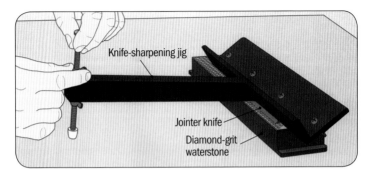

Knife-sharpening jig

Jointer knife

Diamond-grit waterstone

Sharpening the knife

Set a sharpening stone on a flat, smooth work surface; illustrations on this page show a diamond-grit waterstone. To adjust the jig so the beveled edge of the jointer knife is flat on the stone, turn the jig over, rest the bevel on the stone, and turn the wing nuts at the other end of the jig *(above)*. Lubricate the stone—in this case with water—and slide the knife back and forth. Holding the knob-end of the jig flat on the work surface and pressing the knife on the stone, move the jig in a figure-eight pattern *(below)*. Continue until the bevel is flat and sharp. Carefully remove the knife from the jig and hone the flat side of the knife to remove any burr formed in the sharpening process.

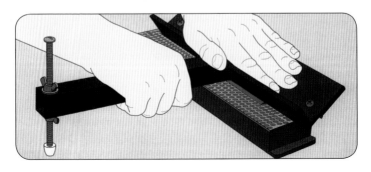

SHARPENING JOINTER
KNIVES *(continued)*

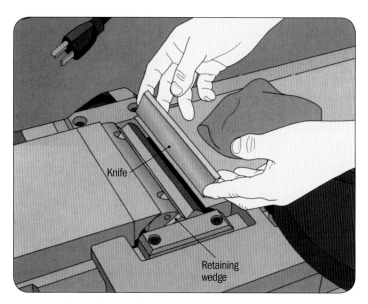

Knife

Retaining
wedge

Reinstalling the knife in the jointer

Insert the retaining wedge in the cutterhead, centering it in the slot with
its grooved edge facing up. With the beveled edge of the knife facing the
outfeed table, slip it between the retaining wedge and the front edge of
the slot, leaving the bevel protruding from the cutterhead.

SHARPENING JOINTER
KNIVES *(continued)*

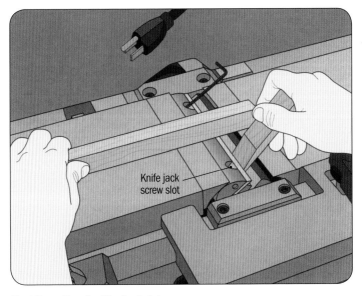

Knife jack
screw slot

Setting the knife height

Adjust the height of the knife using a commercial jig *(page 27)*, or do the job
by hand, as shown above. Cover the edge of the knife with a rag and partially
tighten each lock screw on the retaining wedge. Use a small wooden wedge
to rotate the cutterhead until the edge of the knife is at its highest point—also
known as Top Dead Center or TDC. Then, holding the cutterhead stationary
with a wedge, place a straight hardwood board on the outfeed table so
it extends over the cutterhead. The knife should just brush against the board
along the knife's entire length. If not, use a hex wrench to adjust the knife
jack screws. Once the knife is at the correct height, tighten the lock screws on
the retaining wedge fully, beginning with the one in the center and working out
toward the edges. Sharpen and install the remaining knives the same way.

INSTALLING JOINTER KNIVES WITH A JIG

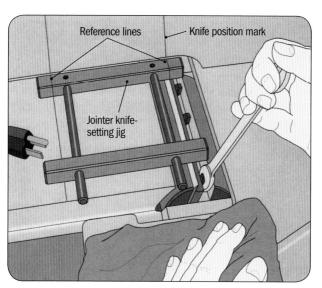

Reference lines — Knife position mark

Jointer knife-setting jig

Using a knife-setting jig

The jig shown above features magnetic arms that will hold a jointer knife at the correct height while you tighten the retaining wedge lock screws. Insert the knife in the cutterhead and position it at its highest point as you would to install the knife by hand *(page 70)*. Then mark a line on the fence directly above the cutting edge. Position the knife-setting jig on the outfeed table, aligning the reference line on the jig arm with the marked line on the fence, as shown. Mark another line on the fence directly above the second reference line on the jig arm. Remove the jig and extend this line across the outfeed table. (The line will help you quickly position the jig the next time you install a knife.) Reposition the jig on the table, aligning its reference lines with the marked lines on the fence. Then use a wrench to tighten the lock screws *(above)*.

SHARPENING PLANER KNIVES

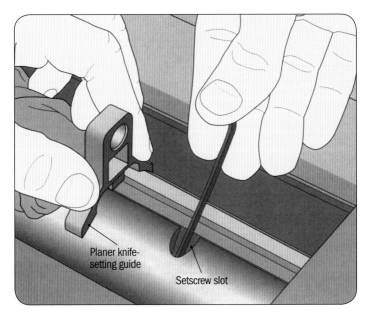

Planer knife-
setting guide

Setscrew slot

Removing and installing a planer knife

Remove a planer knife from the machine and sharpen it as you would a
jointer knife *(page 66)*. To reinstall the knife, use the knife-setting guide
supplied with the machine or a commercially available model like the
one shown on page 62. Place the knife in the planer cutterhead and
partially tighten the setscrews. Hold the knife-setting guide beside one
of the set-screws so that its two feet are resting on the cutterhead on
each side of the opening. Then adjust the setscrew with a hex wrench
until the edge of the knife contacts the bottom of the guide *(above)*.
Repeat for the remaining setscrews.

GLUING JOINTED AND PLANED WOOD

Lumber is seldom available in planks wide enough for a tabletop or a carcase panel; sometimes it cannot be found thick enough for a specific task—a table leg, for example. Often, when you can find such stock, it is prohibitively expensive. To compensate for these shortcomings, woodworkers glue individual boards together. Panels are constructed from edge-to-edge butt joints, as shown below. Leg blanks are made by face gluing boards (page 77). Provided the mating surfaces have been jointed smooth and square, and the proper gluing and clamping techniques are followed, the results are strong and durable. In fact, a well-assembled edge-to-edge or face-to-face butt joint provides a sturdier bond than the wood fibers themselves.

Before edge-gluing boards, arrange the stock so the face of the panel will be visually interesting. The panel should create the illusion of a single piece of wood rather than a composite. To minimize warping, most woodworkers arrange the pieces so the end grain of adjacent boards faces opposite directions (page 76). Use a pencil to mark the end grain orientation on each board.

A jointer produces a smooth, straight, even edge. Gluing jointed boards together edge-to-edge forms a panel every bit as strong as a single piece of lumber.

EDGE GLUING

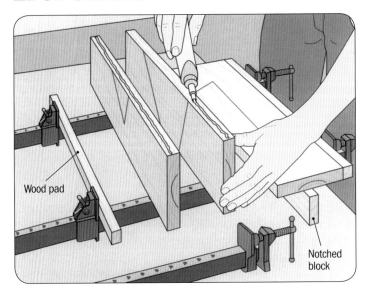

Wood pad

Notched block

Applying the glue

Set two bar clamps on a work surface and lay the boards on top. Use as many clamps as you need to support the pieces at 24- to 36-inch intervals. Keep the bars upright by placing them in notched wood blocks. Arrange the stock to enhance its appearance, making sure the end grain of the boards runs in alternate directions. With the pieces butted edge-to-edge, mark a triangle on the stock to help you rearrange the boards at glue up. Next cut two protective wood pads at least as long as the boards. Leaving the first board face down, stand the other pieces on edge with the triangle marks facing away from you. Apply a thin glue bead to each edge *(above)*, then use a small, stiff-bristled brush to spread the adhesive evenly.

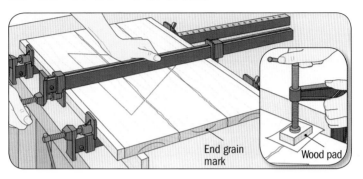

End grain
mark

Wood pad

Tightening the clamps

Set the boards face down and line up their ends, making sure the sides
of the triangle align. Tighten the clamps under the boards just enough
to press them together. Install a third clamp across the top center of
the stock. Finish tightening the clamps *(above)* until there are no gaps
between the boards and a thin bead of glue squeezes out of the joints.
To level adjacent boards that do not lie perfectly flush with each other,
use a C clamp and a wood pad centered over the joint near the end of
the boards; use a strip of wax paper to prevent the pad from sticking to
the boards. Then tighten the clamp until the boards are aligned *(inset)*.

FACE GLUING

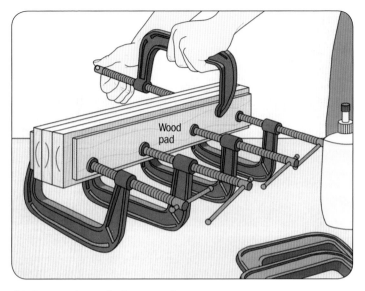

Wood pad

Gluing up boards face-to-face

Cut your stock slightly longer and wider than necessary to enable you to square the blank if the boards shift during glue-up. Lay out the boards face-to-face, alternating the end grain of the pieces and arranging the stock to maximize grain and color. Spread glue on one mating surface of each joint, then use C clamps to hold the pieces together. Starting near the ends of the boards, space the clamps at 3- to 4-inch intervals; protect the stock with wood pads. Tighten the clamps just enough to press the boards together. Turn the assembly over so it sits on the first row of clamps and install a second row along the other edge *(above)*. Finish tightening all the clamps until there are no gaps between the boards and a thin glue bead squeezes out of the joints.

Index

INDEX

Index

THE *Missing* SHOP MANUAL SERIES

THE *Missing* SHOP MANUAL

LATHE

THE *Missing* SHOP MANUAL

DRILLS *and* DRILL PRESSES

THE *Missing* SHOP MANUAL

ROUTER

THE *Missing* SHOP MANUAL

GLUE *and* CLAMPS

THE *Missing* SHOP MANUAL

CIRCULAR SAWS *and* JIG SAWS

THE *Missing* SHOP MANUAL

TABLE SAW

Lathe
ISBN 978-1-56523-470-3
$12.95 USD • 152 Pages

Drills and Drill Presses
ISBN 978-1-56523-472-7
$9.95 USD • 104 Pages

Router
ISBN 978-1-56523-489-5
$12.95 • 208 Pages

Glue and Clamps
ISBN 978-1-56523-468-0
$9.95 USD • 104 Pages

Circular Saws and Jig Saws
ISBN 978-1-56523-469-7
$9.95 USD • 88 Pages

Table Saw
ISBN 978-1-56523-471-0
$12.95 USD • 144 Pages

These are the manuals that should have come with your new woodworking tools. In addition to explaining the basics of safety and set-up, each *Missing Shop Manual* covers everything your new tool was designed to do on its own and with the help of jigs & fixtures. No fluff; just straight tool information at your fingertips.

Look for These Books at Your Local Bookstore or Woodworking Retailer

To order direct, call **800-457-9112 or** visit *www.FoxChapelPublishing.com*

By mail, please send check or money order + $4.00 per book for S&H to:
Fox Chapel Publishing, 1970 Broad Street, East Petersburg, PA 17520